The Life and Works of Galileo Galilei

Biography 4th Grade
Children's Art Biographies

BABY PROFESSOR

EDUCATION KIDS

Speedy Publishing LLC
40 E. Main St. #1156
Newark, DE 19711
www.speedypublishing.com

In this book, we're going to talk about the life of astronomer Galileo Galilei. So let's get right to it!

WHO WAS GALILEO GALILEI?

Galileo was an Italian scientist, mathematician, and astronomer who is best known for using the telescope and recording his observations about the planets and stars.

GALILEO

During his time, it was thought that the Earth was at the center of the solar system and the universe. Galileo challenged those beliefs. He believed that the sun was the center of our solar system

Using experimental science to challenge long-held beliefs made the Catholic Church very nervous. They wanted religion to control people's beliefs, not science. They wanted to silence Galileo from expressing his thoughts and findings.

EARLY LIFE

Born in Pisa, Italy in 1564, Galileo was the first child born to Vincenzo and Giulia Galilei who eventually had six children together. His father was well-known as a musician and also as a music theorist.

At the age of 10, they moved to Florence and while there Galileo began his studies at the Camaldolese monastery. At the age of 19 he went back to the Pisa to become a doctor and entered the University of Pisa. He was intrigued by the subjects he was learning and especially by physics and mathematics.

At that time, the view of the world as described by Aristotle, the Greek philosopher and scientist who lived about three centuries before Christ, was the established "scientific" view. It was the only view supported by the Catholic Church.

At the beginning, Galileo didn't question this belief. He was working toward becoming a professor at the university. Unfortunately, in 1585 he couldn't continue his studies due to financial problems and he left the university.

CAREER IN ACADEMICS

Even though he left his formal studies, Galileo kept teaching himself from mathematical and scientific books. He supported himself with tutoring and teaching as best he could. During this time he started to do an in-depth study of objects in motion.

GALILEO GALILEI

He published a book called The Little Balance. This book was about hydrostatic principles, which simply means it was about the pressures that are exerted by liquids due to the force of gravity when they are at rest. It was about how to weigh small quantities using these principles. The book brought some fame to Galileo and as a result he was offered a teaching position at the University of Pisa.

During this time, Galileo came up with the idea for an interesting experiment. He wanted to prove that two objects with different masses would fall with the same acceleration and hit the ground at the same time. Aristotle had claimed that objects would fall at a speed that was relative to their mass.

GALILEVS
GALILEVS
MATHVS:

A student of Galileo's claimed that he went up to the top of the leaning tower of Pisa to test his theory. He dropped two spheres of unequal mass and found that he was right. They hit the ground at exactly the same time.

As Galileo continued his experiments, he recorded his findings and published them in a book called Du Moto, which means "on motion." As Galileo became more and more confident about his findings, he criticized Aristotle's views openly. This didn't make him popular and his teaching contract with the university wasn't renewed.

Galileo pushed forward and found a new position to teach geometry and astronomy at the University of Padua. His father had passed away in 1591 and he needed to take care of his younger brother. He taught at the University of Padua for 18 years. He became known for his exciting well-attended lectures, which increased his fame.

GALILEO'S FINDINGS

Galileo continued his scientific experiments. He developed a balance used to measure small objects that was based on the hydrostatic principles he had discovered. He also continued to refine his thoughts and theories on the motion of falling objects and the law of acceleration.

He began to say openly that the astronomer Copernicus was correct when he had stated that the Earth revolved around the sun, as opposed to Aristotle's view that the Earth was at the center. In 1604, he published more of his findings in a book called The Operations of the Geometrical and Military Compass.

USING A TELESCOPE

In 1609, Galileo found out about a telescope that had been built by eyeglass makers in the Netherlands. He soon created a telescope of his own and gave a demonstration of its powers to some merchants in Venice. The merchants thought the telescope was useful to spot ships and gave Galileo some money to create some for them.

Galileo saw another use for his telescope as well. It could be used to look at the moon and planets. As he looked into his telescope, night after night, he found that the moon wasn't flat, it had craters and mountains just like Earth. He also found that Venus showed up in phases just like the moon. This proved that Venus was in orbit around the Sun. He also found that the planet Jupiter had moons that revolved around it.

Little by little Galileo and his telescope were giving evidence to the fact that Aristotle and the Catholic Church couldn't be correct about the nature of Earth's position in the universe and that Copernicus who had lived and worked in the late 1400s during the Renaissance was correct.

In 1613, after finding a way to observe the sun with his telescope, he discovered sunspots, which disproved Aristotle's views that the sun was perfect. He wrote a letter to a student in which he outlined why the theories of Copernicus were not heresy.

THE CATHOLIC CHURCH REACTS

When the letter that Galileo had written to his student became public, the Church came down hard on Galileo. They told him that he was not to teach or defend Copernican theory. Galileo didn't want to go to war with the Church. After all, he was a Catholic himself. He obeyed the Church for seven years, at least in public.

In 1623, Cardinal Maffeo Barberini became Pope Urban VIII. The new pope was a friend of Galileo's, so Galileo was allowed to continue his work in astronomy. He even encouraged him to publish his work as long as it gave equal respect to the theories of both Aristotle and Copernicus. In 1632, the Dialogue Concerning the Two Chief World Systems was published. Galileo had described both theories in the book but the way he wrote it, it wasn't impartial at all. He had made Aristotle's views look like the work of a fool. He had made his friend the pope look foolish too.

Galileo had pushed the Church to their breaking point. He was summoned to appear in Rome. After a series of inquisitions, the Church threatened Galileo with torture if he didn't change his beliefs. He was formally convicted of heresy against the Church and spent the remaining nine years of his life under house arrest.

He was ordered not to have any visitors at his home. He's also ordered not to publish any further works about his theories. He chooses to ignore both commands and continues to publish his work. During this time, he wrote the book, Two New Sciences, which was a summary of all the work he had done in his lifetime on the science of motion and also on the strength of materials. This important manuscript and others were not published in Italy, but instead in Holland in the year 1638.

The stress of all he had been through took its toll on Galileo's health and by now he was in his seventies. The man who was the first to see the craters of the moon was now nearly blind. Despite all this, he continued to work. A year before he passed away he designed a pendulum that was used for keeping time.

THE LEGACY OF GALILEO

Galileo died near Florence, Italy in January of 1642, after a severe fever and heart troubles. He was 78 years old. In time, the Church changed its views about science. Eventually it lifted the ban on most of the publications that supported the Copernican theory.

By 1835, almost 200 years after Galileo's death, it dropped its opposition to the sun being the center of the solar system. It took even longer for the Church to express regrets over the way this great scientist had been treated.

In 1992, Pope John Paul II expressed his sadness over the way Galileo's views had been handled by the Church. Galileo's observations about our solar system backed up by his mathematical and scientific knowledge changed the world's understanding of the universe.

He developed scientific experiments and used logical thinking as well as solid mathematics to prove his theories. He played a major role in the progression of the scientific method as a way to learn about our universe. He's earned the title that so many historians have given to him—"The Father of Modern Science."

Awesome! Now you know about the amazing knowledge that Galileo contributed to the world. You can find more Science Biography books from Baby Professor by searching the website of your favorite book retailer.

Visit

BABY PROFESSOR
EDUCATION KIDS

www.BabyProfessorBooks.com

to download Free Baby Professor eBooks and view
our catalog of new and exciting Children's Books

Made in the USA
Middletown, DE
09 October 2018